# Easter Coloring book
# JESUS LIVES!

Illustrated by

Deb Johnson

The purchase of this coloring book grants you the rights to photocopy the contents for classroom use.
Notice: It is unlawful to copy these pages for resale purposes. Copy permission is for private use only.

warner press
KiDs

M000114626

305800213937

Jesus is God's only Son.
God sent Jesus to the world as a baby.

# When He grew up, Jesus taught people about God.

# Jesus healed people when they were sick, too.

Then Jesus had to go to Jerusalem.
"Bring a donkey for Me to ride,"
He told His disciples.

When people saw Jesus, they waved palm branches.
"Hosanna!" they shouted.

Some bad men did not like Jesus.
They planned to kill Him.

# Jesus and His disciples ate a special meal called Passover.

# Then Jesus went into the garden to pray.

# Soldiers came and took Jesus away.
## They put a crown of thorns on His head.

# Jesus had to carry a heavy wooden cross to a lonely hill.

Soldiers nailed Jesus to the cross. Jesus prayed,
"Father, forgive them. They do not know
what they are doing."

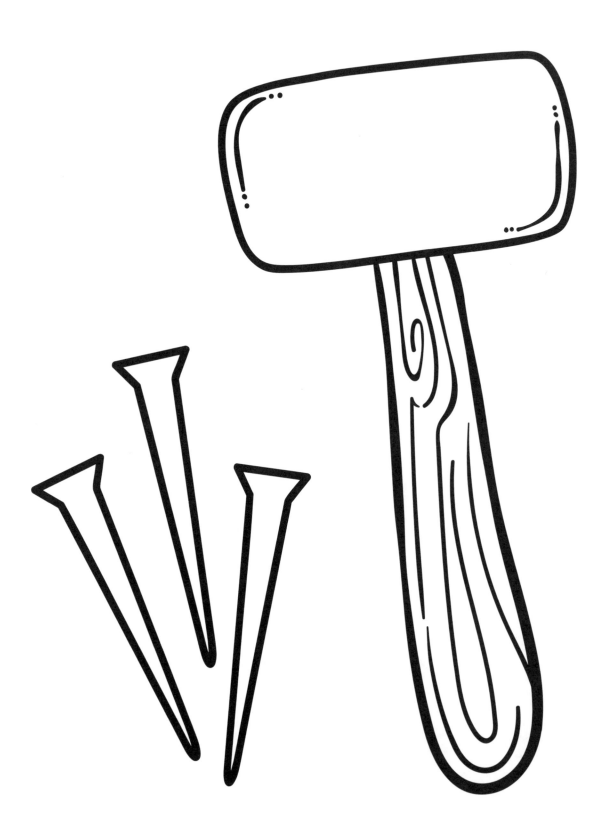

Then Jesus died. His body was put in a tomb, and a huge stone was rolled in front of the door.

Later, Jesus' friends came to put spices
and perfume on His body.

The stone was rolled away, and an angel
was sitting on it. He said,
"Jesus is not here. He has risen!"

# The women ran to tell the good news.
## JESUS IS ALIVE!

*Go quickly, and tell his disciples that he is risen from the dead.*
**MATTHEW 28:7**